MUSICIANS INSTITUTE
Rock Lead BASICS

by Nick Nolan and Danny Gill

To access audio visit:
www.halleonard.com/mylibrary

6295-7073-0083-2974

ISBN 978-0-7935-7378-3

HAL•LEONARD®
CORPORATION
7777 W. BLUEMOUND RD. P.O. BOX 13819 MILWAUKEE, WI 53213

Visit Hal Leonard Online at
www.halleonard.com

Contents

CHAPTER 1

GETTING STARTED

We'd like to start you off with your lead playing the same way we got started—by diving right into some licks.

The licks presented in this chapter use some common techniques like *bending* and *vibrato.* These techniques will be explained in depth later, but for now, just read the transcriptions and listen to the audio tracks. All of these licks work in the key of A.

Notice there's a *bend* on the fifth note in figure 1. When you hit that note, push the string up (towards the ceiling) and let it back down. Try to shake the last note up and down—this is called *vibrato.*

2 ◆ **Fig. 1**

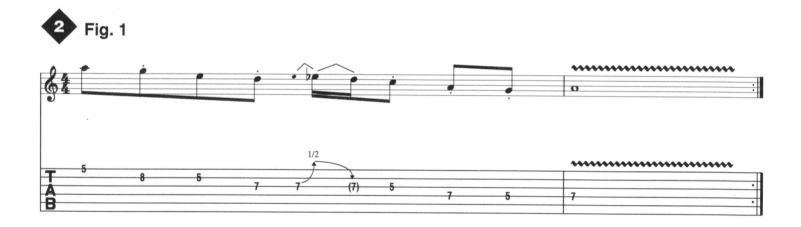

This next lick uses two bends, the second of which is held (last note). Vibrato is also added on this final note. Shake it up and down as before, but try to keep it centered near the original bend.

3 ◆ **Fig. 2**

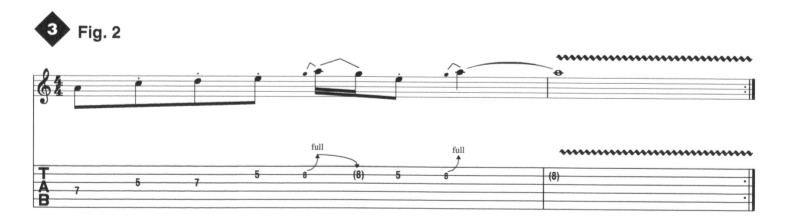

Now let's try a *slide*. A slide is when you hit a note and slide up or down to your next note. The trick is, don't pick the note you're sliding to.

◆4 Fig. 3

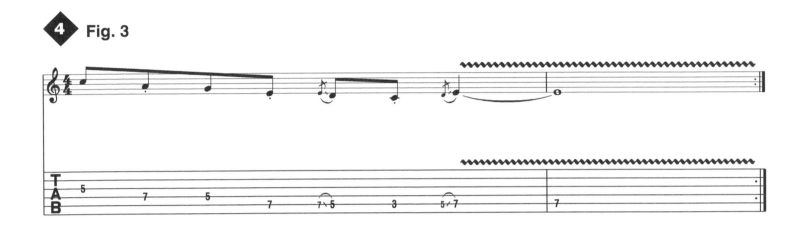

The lick in figure 4, below, winds around the root (A) before finally coming to rest, or *resolving,* on the A5 chord.

◆5 Fig. 4

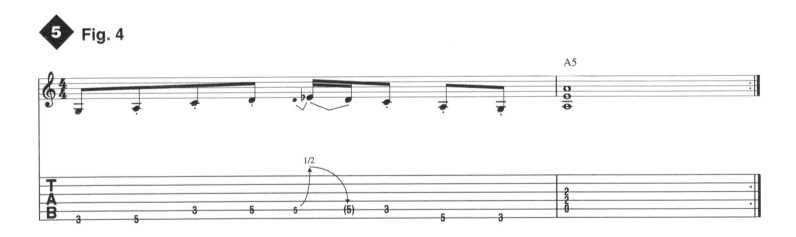

Track **6** combines figres 1, 2, 3, and 4 to create a short solo. Take your time learning it so you can play it with no mistakes. Then, move on to Chapter 2.

CHAPTER 2

THE MINOR PENTATONIC SCALE

It could be said the minor pentatonic scale lies at the core of rock lead guitar. It seems almost all of the "greats" use this type of scale as the center-point of their playing. The licks you learned in chapter one were all drawn from the A minor pentatonic scale.

There are only five notes in this type of scale. That's why its called *pentatonic* ("penta" means five). The five notes of the minor pentatonic scale are the first, third, fourth, fifth, and seventh notes of the natural minor scale (see chapter 7). Another way to say it is we are leaving out the second and sixth notes of the natural minor scale. By leaving these two notes out, the scale takes on a more "primal" character. The scale has no half steps (notes that are one fret apart), and that alone seems to make the scale more suitable for an aggressive sound.

Below are five different patterns of the minor pentatonic scale. The root (or letter name) of the scale is circled. If, for example, you wanted to play the A minor pentatonic scale using Pattern 4, you would look at Pattern 4 and put any of the circled notes on the note A. I would choose the sixth string circle and put my first finger on the A note at the fifth fret, sixth string. From there, just follow the diagram.

Fig. 5

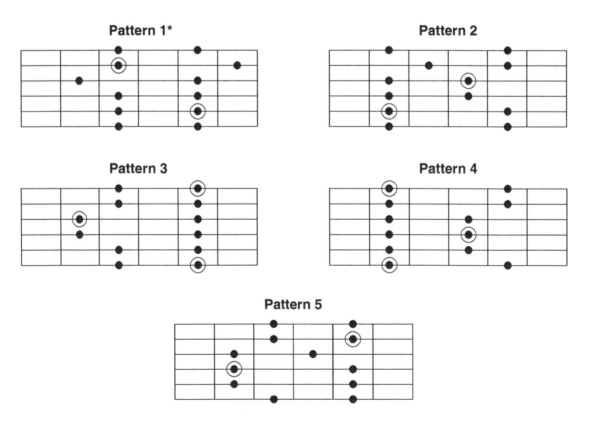

*Note: The pattern numbers 1–5 are are a Musician's Institute standard. They are based on the key of C. For example, the lowest place you can play a C scale is in open position. Therefore, it gets the number 1. Pattern 2 would be the next highest, an so on. Throughout this book and other MI books, this numbering system will be used. It is a good idea to become familiar with it.

Of all these patterns, the one that wins the popularity contest is Pattern 4. Millions of solos have been played out of this pattern. It seems all of the notes fall into a comfortable shape for your hand.

Let's get you started with some of the most common minor pentatonic ideas. These licks should sound familiar; they've been ripped off by almost everybody!

To keep things simple, all of these licks are in E minor (indicated by one sharp—F♯— in the key signature). In each case, they are first performed by the guitar alone, then again with full band.

7 8 Fig. 6

9 10 Fig. 7

11 12 Fig. 8

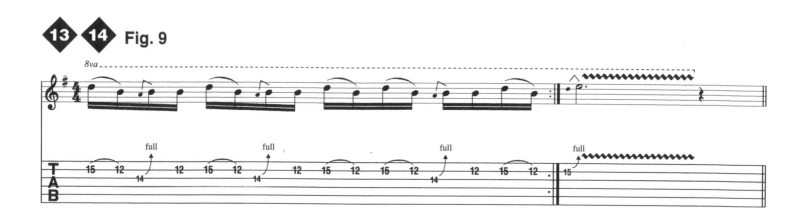

Fig. 9

This next one uses Pattern 2. Although played in a different position, this lick is also in the same key (E minor).

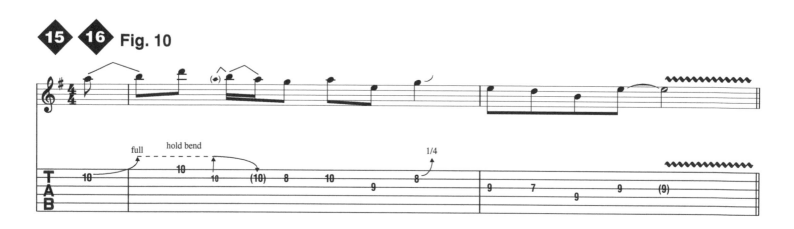

Fig. 10

CONNECTING PENTATONICS

Although it's fine to stay within each of the patterns for your licks, connecting one pattern to another will give you more range from high to low. The following figure shows a useful way of connecting the pentatonic patterns across your neck.

Fig. 11

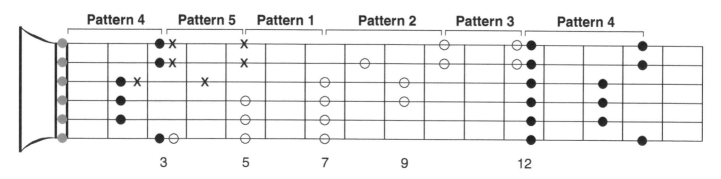

In the above guitar neck, there are symbols that signify the various patterns of E minor pentatonic scale. The "solid dots" represent our good friend, Pattern 4 (notice there are two different octaves of it). The "x'es" represent an option of connecting Pattern 4 to Pattern 5 as demonstrated in Figure 12.

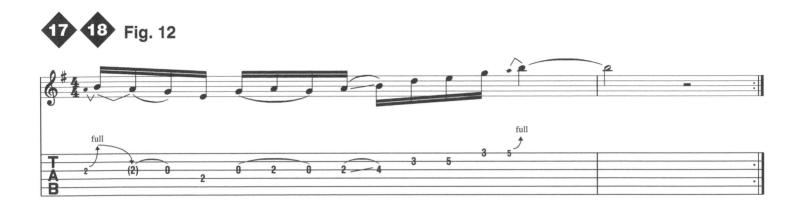

In the guitar neck shown as Figure 11, the "open dots" represent how to connect Patterns 4, 5, 1, and 2, giving you a three–octave range. This is demonstrated in Figure 13.

19 **20** Fig. 13

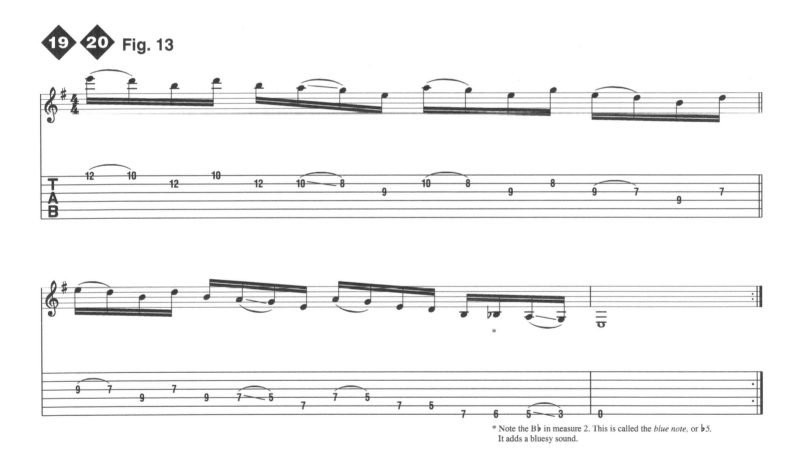

* Note the B♭ in measure 2. This is called the *blue note*, or ♭5. It adds a bluesy sound.

Now that you've learned some licks, take some time to practice them. One good idea could be to turn on a drum machine and keep playing the licks over and over. Try changing some of the notes to see what you can come up with. Having fun is one of the keys to sounding good, so experiment to keep it exciting.

CHAPTER 3

THE MAJOR PENTATONIC SCALE

In this chapter you'll learn about the *major pentatonic scale.* Here's a short–cut: The major pentatonic scale has the same scale shapes as the minor pentatonic scale. This means you won't have to learn any new scales.

You may be thinking, "If the scales shapes are the same, why even learn the major pentatonic scale?" Well, well, well...as you further your studies of music, you'll realize there are two very different worlds—the "major world" and the "minor world." Each "world" needs it's own set of scales for you to be comfortable when soloing. So, let's get an understanding of the difference between major and minor.

Below are the five major pentatonic scale patterns. As I said earlier, the patterns look the same as before. However, the *roots* (circled notes) are different.

Fig. 14

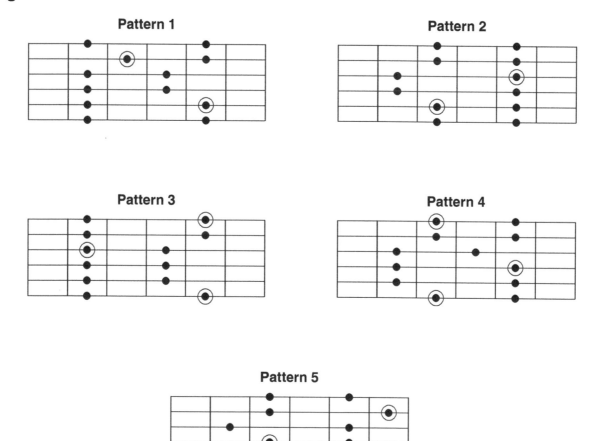

Take notice of our favorite pattern from the last chapter. In minor it's called Pattern 4; in major it's called Pattern 3. For example, Pattern 4 of E minor pentatonic is exactly the same notes as Pattern 3 of G major pentatonic. However (and this is important), the *roots* are different.

If your song is in E minor, you should use the E minor pentatonic scale for soloing. If your song is in G major, you should use the G major pentatonic scale for soloing. What's the difference? The difference is in *the song.* An E minor song feels "at home" on an E minor chord. When you play a song in E minor, the last chord of the song is almost always E minor. When you play a G major song, it feels "at home" in G, and usually ends on a G major chord. This is a concept known as *relative keys:* keys that have exactly the same notes, but have different *roots* (the root is the note that feels "at home").

A lot of rock guitarists use their guitar to figure out the relative keys. The guitar neck below demonstrates how to do this. Your first finger (1) will be your minor root and your fourth finger (4) will be your major root.

Fig. 15

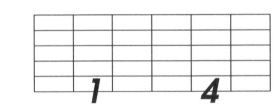

Try this: Put your first finger on the note B (seventh fret of the sixth string). OK, now B is your minor root. Using your fourth finger, tell me what B's relative major is… *(answer: D Major)*

Now put your fourth finger on the note C (eighth fret of the sixth string). OK. Now C is your *major* root (because you're using your fourth finger). Using your first finger tell me what C's relative minor is… *(answer: A Minor).* Get it?

The sound of major pentatonic is a brighter, happier sound than the minor pentatonic. Here are some licks for you to practice, using the D major pentatonic scale patterns.

21 22 **Fig. 16**

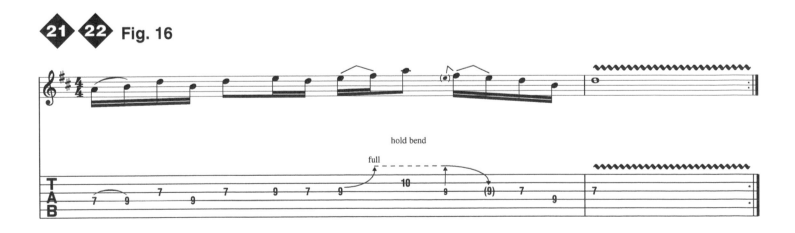

This final lick connects Patterns 1, 2, 3, and 4 by using slides. Sliding between patterns is a great way to connect them.

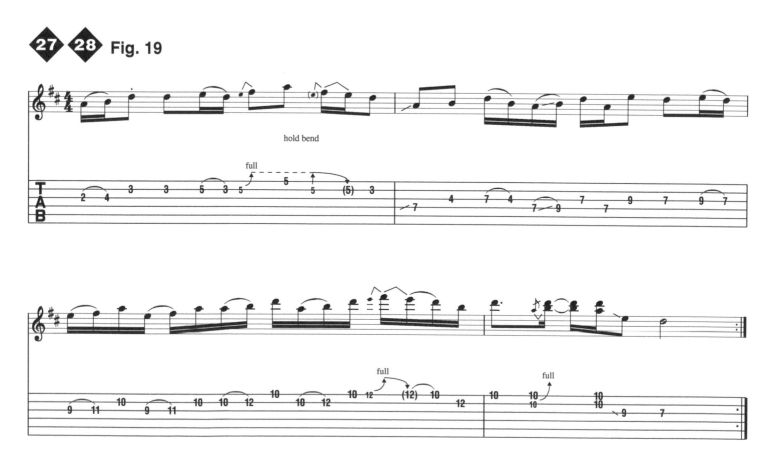

CHAPTER 4

BENDING

Before we get any further along on the subject of *which* notes to play, it's time to talk about *how* to play them. Bending and vibrato are pretty "mature" subjects. In many people's opinion, the difference between an amateur and a pro is *not* the amount of licks or the speed, but the bending and vibrato. Your ears are the most important learning resource here. The more you listen, the more you learn. So pay close attention to how things *sound* on the audio. In fact, pay close attention to how things sound on all recordings.

The technique behind bending notes will vary from guitarist to guitarist. But most rock players use a similar technique which involves the wrist. What this means is that you're not going to use any finger movement to bend the notes. You'll lock your fingers in place and by turning your wrist; you'll push or pull the note to get your bend. Yes, I said push *or* pull–depending on which string you are bending. Sometimes you will push the string toward the ceiling, while other times you will pull the string toward the floor.

Pushing up

Pulling down

Most players tend to favor pushing the note up. That's easy to do on all strings except the fifth and sixth strings. If you push those strings up, they might go off the fingerboard.

The bending rule: Always use as many fingers as possible to make a bend. For example, if you're using your third finger to bend a note, put your first and second fingers in behind the third to give the bend more strength. Look at the series of pictures below. Notice how the fingers remain locked while the wrist twists to push up the string. Also, the fingers are pushing *under* the fourth and fifth strings so they don't get caught in the bend and add extra noise.

Preparing to bend

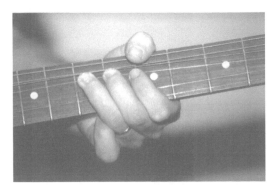
Executing bend

Another consideration in bending is to bend away from your next note. Look at figure 20 below. We are bending a note on the third string and our next note is on the second string. In this case, you should bend the third string up and away from the second string. This figure is also a good exercise for "tuning" your bend. The bent note and the fretted note should have the same pitch. Practice this until you've got it.

29 **Fig. 20**

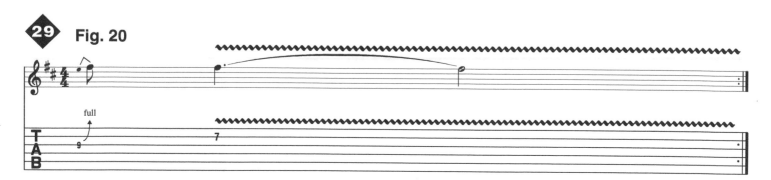

COMMON BENDING IDEAS

Here are some bending licks all rock guitarists should know. They all use a full bend. A full bend is the equivalent of two frets distance (also called a *whole step).* The key for each figure is B minor.

30 **31** **Fig. 21**

32 **33** **Fig. 22**

34 **35** **Fig. 23**

BLUESY BENDS

These next three licks use an interesting bend. The distance of the bend is a *half step* (the equivalent of one fret). It's easy to over-bend a half step. Try bending a whole step, then a half step. Master the difference. The thing that's interesting in figure 24 is the note we'll be bending. It's called the third—meaning the third note of the diatonic scale. Since we're in the key of B minor, the third note is D. When you bend the third up a half step, you get a *bluesy* sound. In fact, it's best to use these ideas when the band plays a dominant seventh chord. The dominant seventh chord is the main chord for blues. Note: The half-step bend in figure 24 is best pulled down, while the full bend should be pushed up. Again, the key is B minor.

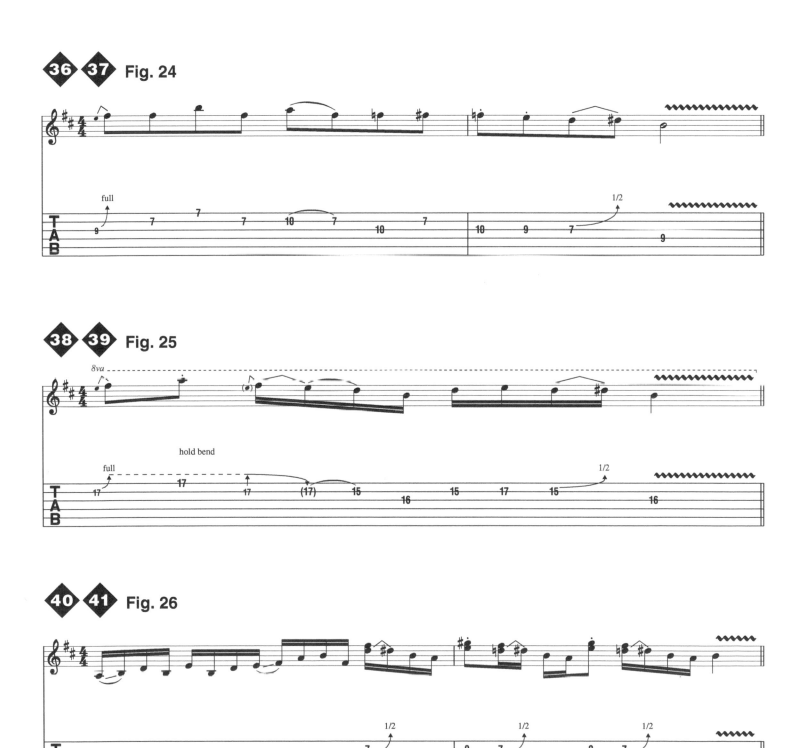

THE MINOR THIRD BEND

As with the last bend, this bend takes a bit of control. It's called a *minor third bend.* To understand this, you need to know a minor third is a three fret distance (also called 1 1/2 steps). Try the licks below and concentrate on the tuning of your bend.

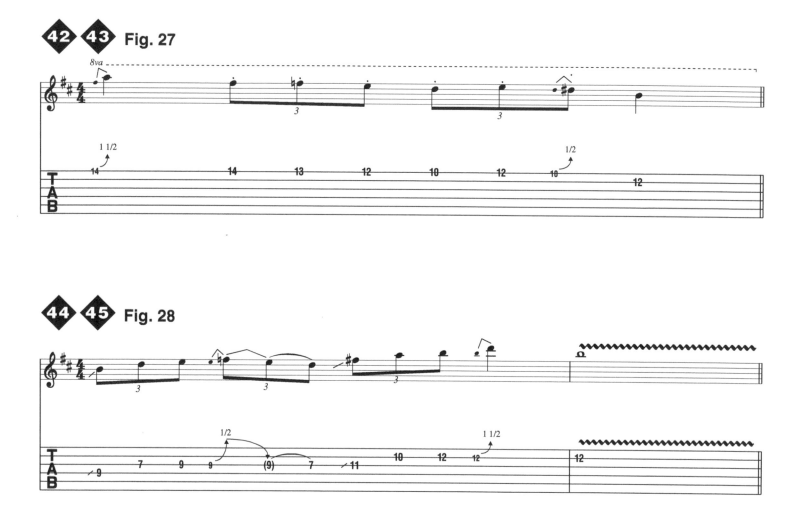

CHAPTER 5

PENTATONIC JAMMING

Now that you've got your scales, licks, and some skills under your belt, it's time to put everything together and see what we get.

In this chapter, we have two chord progressions well-suited for pentatonic soloing along with two sample solos. On the audio, you will first hear the progression played once, with the solo. You should learn the solo note–for–note so you can play along. Following this, another track plays through the same progession four times without the solo, so you can try out all of your new ideas.

This first progression is a straight ahead rock tune. The tempo's not too fast, so you should be able to work in a lot of your new licks. The key is somewhat hard to name theoretically. A lot of rock players would say, "This is in A," because the A chord sounds "at home." And for the purpose of this book, I'm going to tell you, "This is in A." In later books, we'll go into more depth with the theory behind chord progressions.

Check this out: Even though I told you this is in A, at times I use scales other than the A minor pentatonic scale. On the E chord I use the E minor pentatonic scale and on the G chord I use the G major pentatonic scale. This is commonly called "covering the changes." This means you are following the names of the chords with your scales. (A chord = A scale, E chord = E scale, and so on...) It's not something you *have* to do, but it's fun, sounds good, and is also challenging.

46 **Fig. 29 – Pentatonic Solo 1**

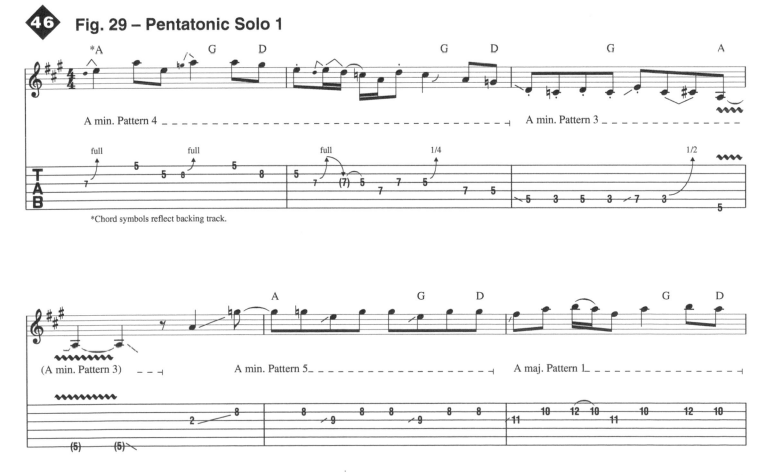

*Chord symbols reflect backing track.

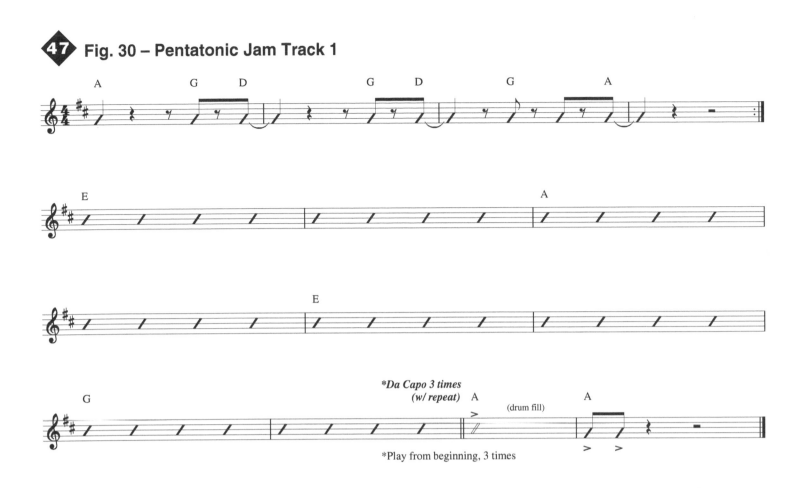

47 **Fig. 30 – Pentatonic Jam Track 1**

Our next jam is an uptempo tune in B. Even though it has two sections, I am using B minor pentatonic Pattern 4 all the way through.

Because the tempo is so fast, I start off slowly, in order to let the rhythm "breathe" a little. Notice how cool it sounds to repeat a riff as the chords move underneath you. This sets up the last lick in the final two measures.

48 **Fig. 31 – Pentatonic Solo 2**

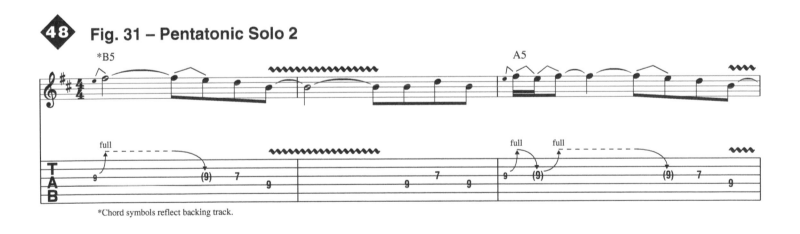

*Chord symbols reflect backing track.

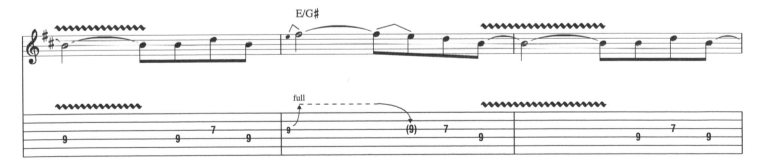

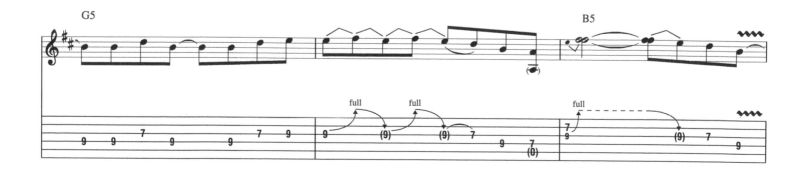

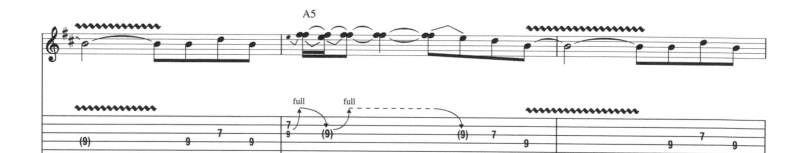

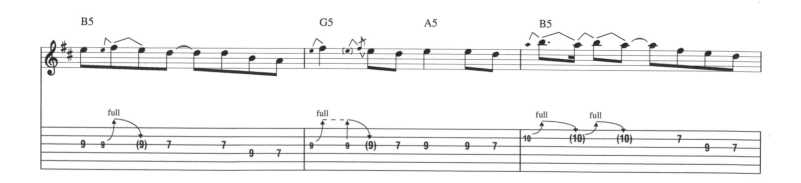

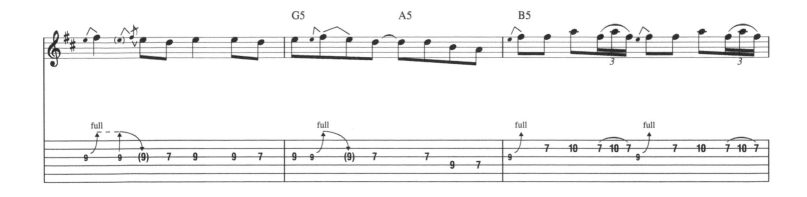

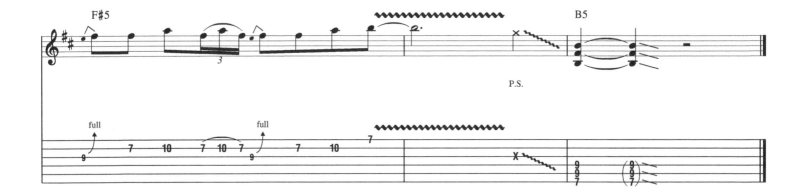

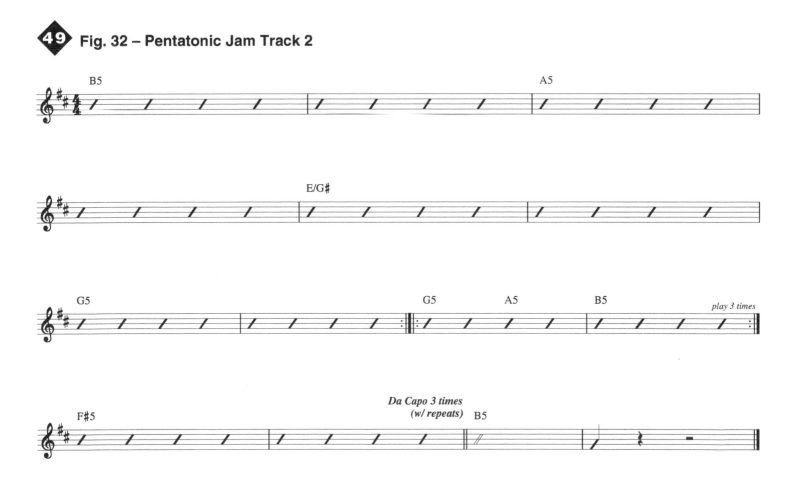

49 **Fig. 32 – Pentatonic Jam Track 2**

CHAPTER 6

VIBRATO

Ever hear someone play one note on the guitar that made you just turn your head and say, *"Yeah!"*? Chances are it was because of a great vibrato. Vibrato is when you shake a note up and down to make it "sing." That's it. But it is easier said than done.

The best teacher for improving your vibrato is your ear. You have to listen closely to yourself and really analyze your sound. Keeping all of that in mind, let's try a few exercises.

Start by placing your first finger on the twelfth fret of the G string (see picture). Using a metronome, shake the note G in even eighth notes first. Then we'll try it in sixteenth notes, triplets, and finally, sixteenth-note triplets. Each time, the natural tension of the string should bring you back "home" to the note of G.

50 Fig. 33

51 Fig. 34

52 Fig. 35

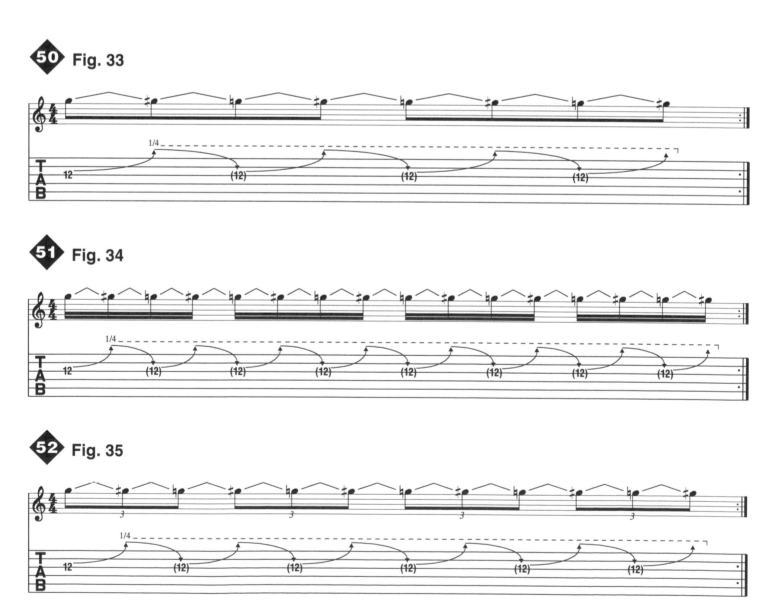

22

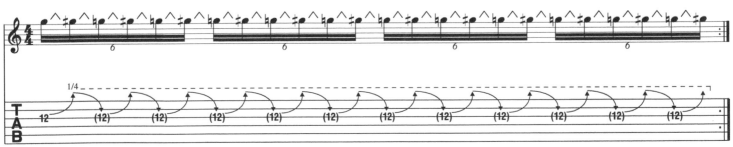

Now try each of these exercises with your second, third, and fourth fingers. Make sure you are using your wrist to move your fingers.

Using the second finger

Using the third finger

Using the fourth finger

In this next exercise, we are going to descend a C major scale using a slow, heavy vibrato timed in sixteenth notes.

54 **Fig. 37**

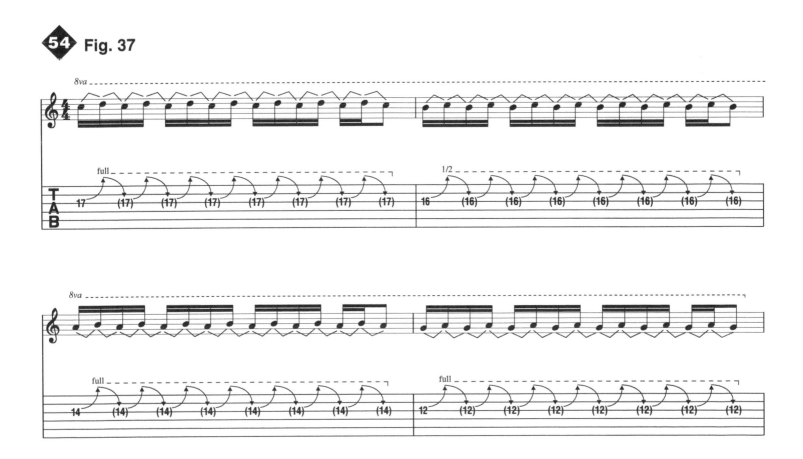

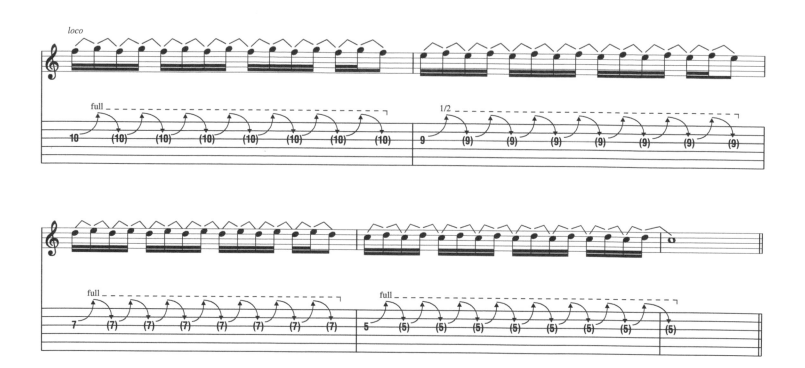

The most difficult vibrato is when you add vibrato to a bend. In the next exercise, we are going to bend into the note E of the C major scale, and then add vibrato, again timed in sixteenth notes.

Start by bending with your third finger, then try it with each of your other fingers. Each picture shows the same bend using a different finger. Check out how the first finger is being bent toward the floor, while the second, third, and fourth fingers bend upwards. This downward bend gives the first finger some extra strength when bending whole steps on the G string.

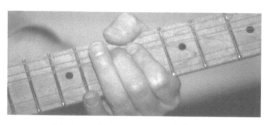

Using the first finger

Using the second finger

Using the third finger

Using the fourth finger

55 ◆ **Fig. 38**

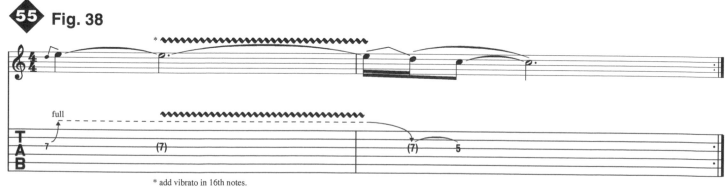

* add vibrato in 16th notes.

Here is a short blues in C minor. In this exercise, you are going to be using your first, second, and third fingers to add vibrato. Notice how the speed of the vibrato varies—listen closely.

56 **Fig. 39 – Blues in C Minor**

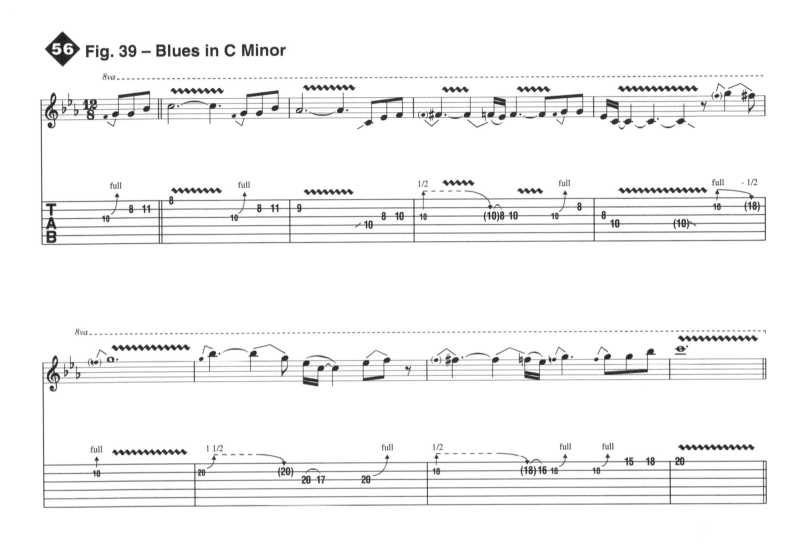

As you become more comfortable with your vibrato, try practicing with each of these different embellishments: slow vibrato, fast vibrato, wide vibrato, narrow vibrato, and moving from no vibrato to slight vibrato.

CHAPTER 7

DIATONIC SCALES

Up to this point we have focused on pentatonic scales. This chapter introduces seven–note, diatonic scales, which will fill in the "gaps" left by the five–note pentatonic scales. With the addition of these two notes, it is possible to create melodic lines and scale runs you could not play with the pentatonic scale alone.

Below are five different patterns for the diatonic major scale and five patterns for the natural minor scale.

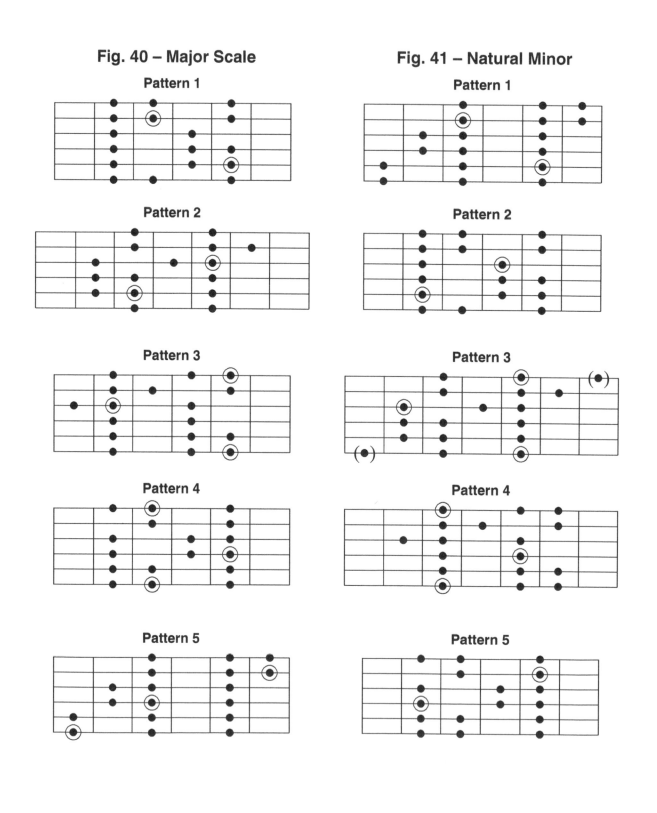

Fig. 40 – Major Scale

Pattern 1

Pattern 2

Pattern 3

Pattern 4

Pattern 5

Fig. 41 – Natural Minor

Pattern 1

Pattern 2

Pattern 3

Pattern 4

Pattern 5

It is important to remember—just like the major and minor pentatonic scales—the diatonic scales also have a relative minor/major relationship.

The rule is: *The relative minor scale begins on the sixth step of the diatonic major scale.* So, for example, C major and A minor are relative. This means C major contains the same notes as A minor.

Fig. 42

C Major:	C	D	E	F	G	A	B	C
	1	2	3	4	5	6	7	8

A Minor:	A	B	C	D	E	F	G	A
	1	2	3	4	5	6	7	8

In figure 43, each " ○ " represents the major scale root, while each " □ " represents the minor scale root.

Fig. 43

Major Pattern 3 / Minor Pattern 4

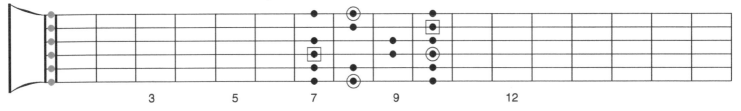

Major Pattern 4 / Minor Pattern 5

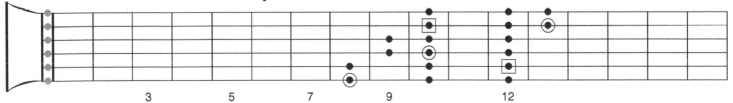

Major Pattern 5 / Minor Pattern 1

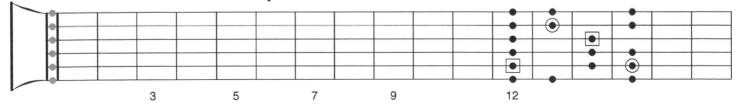

Major Pattern 1 / Minor Pattern 2

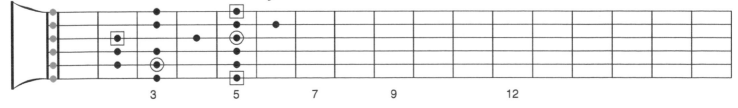

Major Pattern 3 / Minor Pattern 4

The diatonic scale adds two notes within each octave to the pentatonic scale. In A natural minor, these notes are B and F. Let's start our diatonic licks by adding one, or both, of these notes into some rock licks…

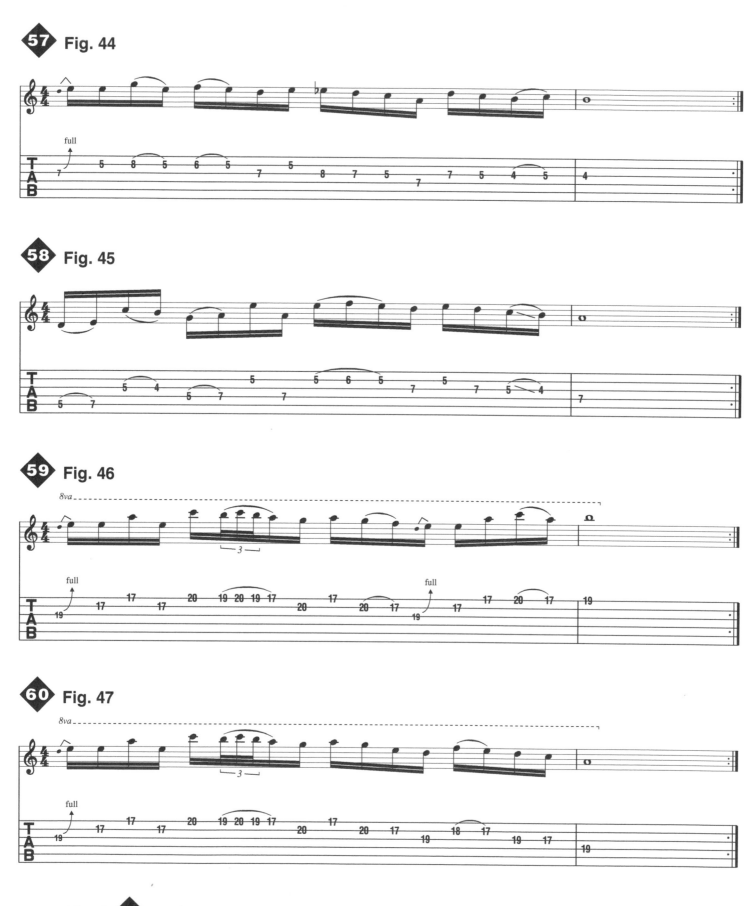

Track **61** combines all of these ideas to create a short solo in A minor.

The next two ideas are great for repeating licks. They are both phrased with *sixteenth–note triplets.* This means there are six notes for every beat.

62 **Fig. 48**

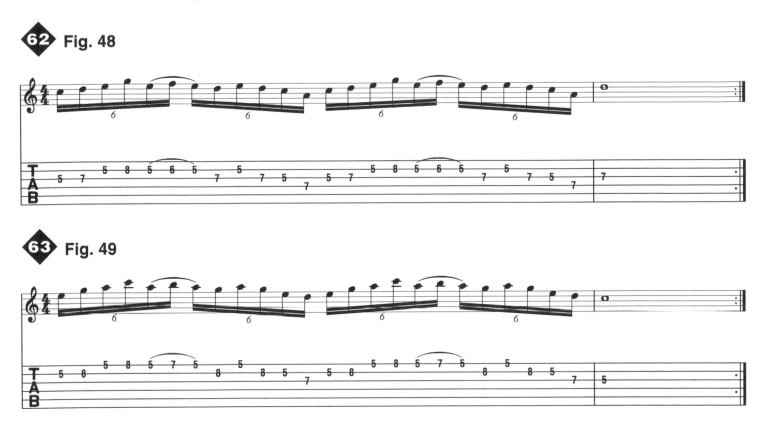

63 **Fig. 49**

64 Now let's connect these two licks over the same chord progression in A minor.

In C major, the diatonic notes added to the pentatonic scale are still B and F. The following exercises use these notes to help move around the neck. Check out the slides.

65 **Fig. 50**

66 **Fig. 51**

67 **Fig. 52**

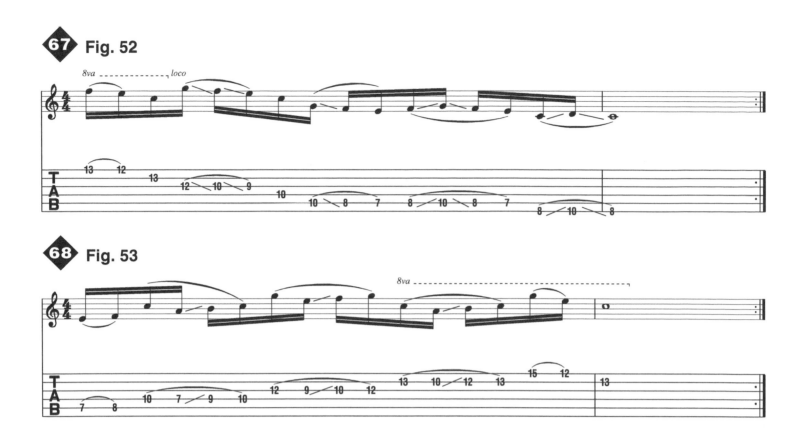

68 **Fig. 53**

69 Now let's connect the previous four licks over a simple chord progression in C major.

The next two ideas cover an even wider range on the neck. Use your pinky to shift positions. Let's try these in the key of A minor.

70 **Fig. 54**

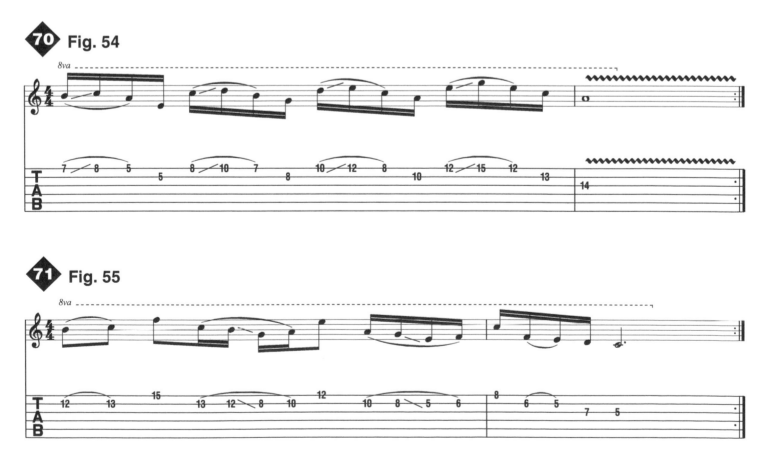

71 **Fig. 55**

Our next lick uses C major Pattern 5. This three–note–per–string scale is great for creating smooth-sounding runs.

72 **Fig. 56**

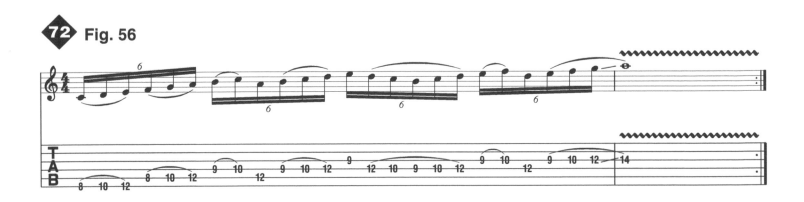

The lick in figure 57 uses a descending idea, combining Patterns 4 and 5 in C major.

73 **Fig. 57**

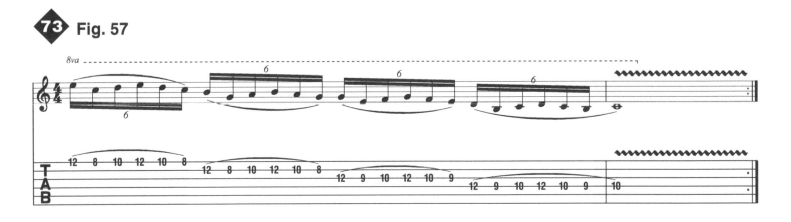

74 Now let's connect the last four licks over a simple chord progression in the key of A minor.

Now you get to try some diatonic ideas yourself. Track **75** will play a single chord progression in A minor like the one you've been hearing. Keep jamming with the track until you play something you like. In the next chapter, we are going to talk about jamming with diatonic scales in much greater detail.

75 **Fig. 58**

CHAPTER 8

DIATONIC JAMMING

Now that you've learned *how* to play diatonic scales, let's focus on *when* to use them.

The first step is to learn the chords of the *harmonized major scale.* This is where it gets a little tough, so follow along closely. The harmonized major scale is a group of chords made from the notes of the diatonic major scale. The order of these chords (which chords are major, minor, or diminished) are the same in every key. Memorize the order in which these chord types occur.

Fig. 59

I	II	III	IV	V	VI	VII
major	minor	minor	major	major	minor	diminished

We are going to be soloing in D major, so let's take a look at the harmonized D major scale:

Fig. 60

D Major	I	II	III	IV	V	VI	VII
	D maj.	E min.	F♯ min.	G maj.	A maj.	B min.	C♯ dim.

Here is an example of diatonic soloing over a progression in D major.

76 **Fig. 61 – Diatonic Solo 1**

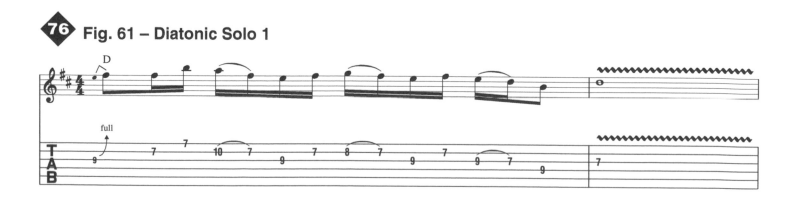

32

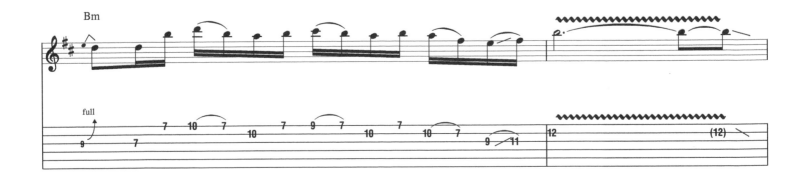

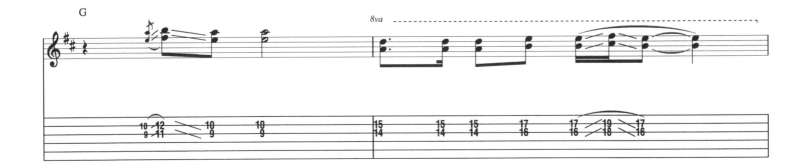

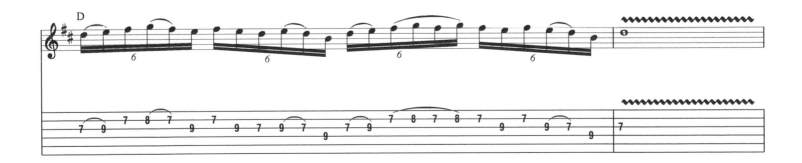

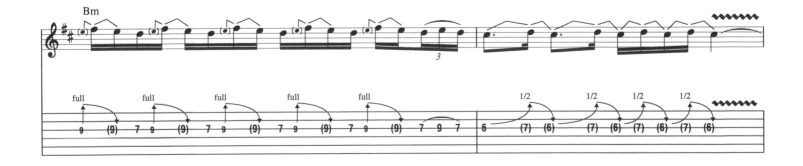

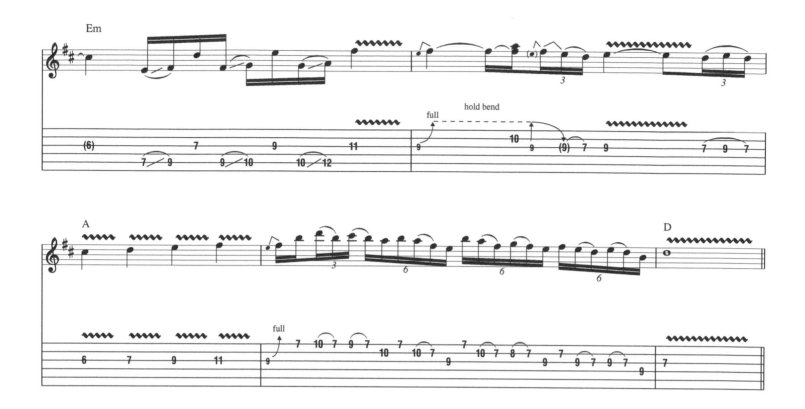

In many rock songs, the first chord gives away its key center. If a song starts on a D major chord (as in figure 61), chances are good it is in the key of D major. Start there and compare the chords of the progression with the chords from the harmonized major scale.

Here is the progression we just soloed over. Take a look at it and compare the analysis of the chords with the chords of the harmonized D major scale (Figure 60).

77 **Fig. 62 – Diatonic Jam Track 1**

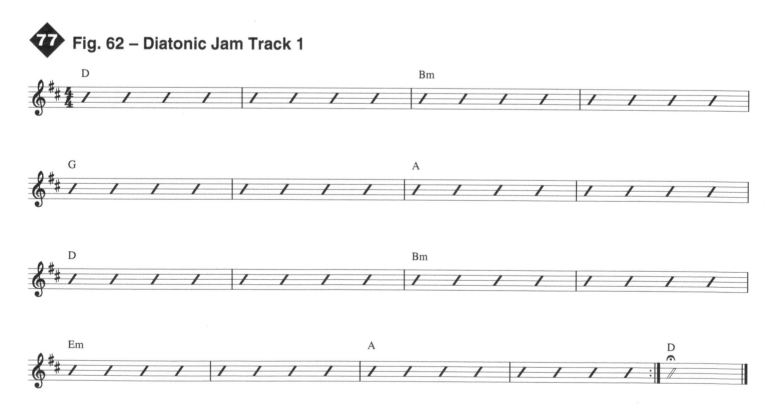

Take time to absorb all of this information before moving on to the minor keys.

Diatonic soloing in minor keys works much the same as in major keys. The first chord is *probably* the key center. Check to see by comparing the chord in a progression with the chords of the harmonized scale. The trick to remember is this: *The natural minor scale starts on the sixth step of its relative diatonic major scale.*

Here are the chords of the harmonized D natural minor scale:

Fig. 63

D Minor	I	II	III	IV	V	VI	VII
	D min.	E dim.	F maj.	G min.	A min.	B♭ maj.	C maj.

Here is an example of diatonic soloing over a progression in D minor.

78 **Fig. 64**

35

This is the progression we just soloed over. If we compare the chords with the harmonized D natural minor scale, we get the following analysis (look at the Roman Numerals). When you're finished analyzing the chords, play through and try out your own solos.

79 **Fig. 65 – Diatonic Jam Track 2**

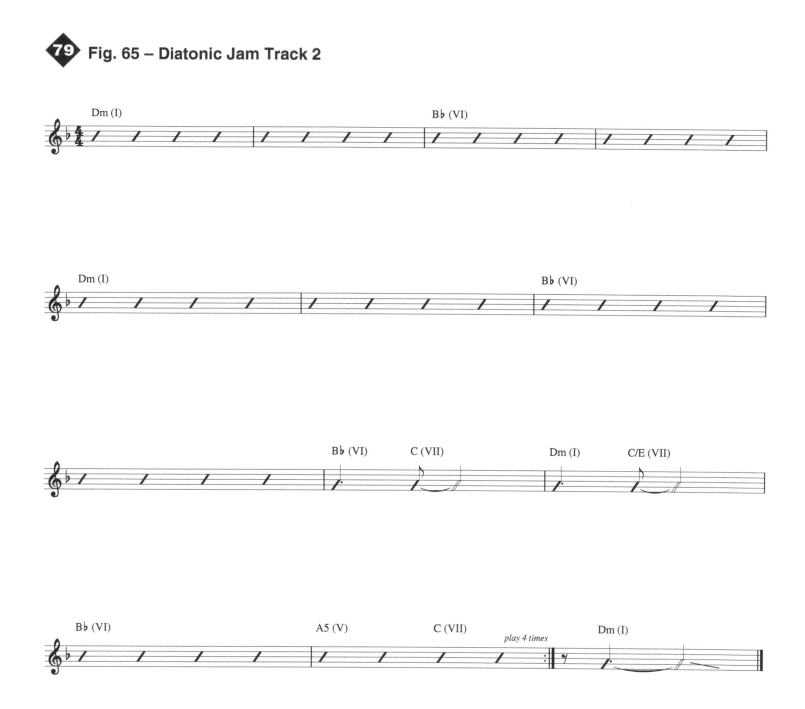

You may have noticed that—in this, our final chapter—we have introduced a little bit of harmony and theory. Go over this information slowly and make sure you absorb all of it before moving on. Not only will it improve your ability to improvise, but it will make you a better overall musician. Also, one last word on pentatonic vs. diatonic scales: Keep in mind that neither scale is "better." It is simply a matter of personal preference. Use your ear to play what you feel. These are just tools to help you get there.

ABOUT THE AUTHORS

Nick Nolan comes from Port Huron, Michigan where he began his professional playing career at the age of sixteen. He then went to G.I.T. on the Eddie Van Halen Scholarship and graduated with honors. After graduating, Nick became an instructor at G.I.T., teaching and writing curriculum for such subjects as: Rock Lead Guitar, Rock Rhythm Guitar, and the Rhythm Section Workshop, as well as teaching Music Reading, Harmony and Theory, Ear Training, and Modern Rock Performance.

Nick is also an active session player in Los Angeles, playing guitar on such T.V. series as: "Melrose Place," "Star Search" (as house guitarist), and "High Tide." You may have also heard Nick on the cartoons: "Bill and Ted's Excellent Adventure," "Back to the Future" (CBS), "Where's Waldo?" (CBS), "Super Mario Brothers" (NBC), "Captain Planet" (FOX), "Exosquad" (Universal), "What a Mess" (DIC), "Don Coyote" (Hanna-Barbera), and "The Funtastic World of Hanna-Barbera."

Nick has also just released his first CD, titled *Up & Down & Back Again* on Standing 8 Records (P.O. Box 5280, North Hollywood, CA 91616)

Danny Gill recorded his first record in 1990 with Hericane Alice (Atlantic Records). Since then, he has gone on to record and tour with Arcade, V.D., Medicine Wheel, and is currently working with his new band, Floor. His songs have appeared on numerous network T.V. shows and major motion picture soundtracks. Danny also teaches guitar at the world famous Musicians Institute in Hollywood, California. His classes include Rock Lead Guitar, Rock Rhythm Guitar, and the Hard Rock Live Playing Workshop, where he specializes in the *heavy stuff.*

CREDITS

Danny Gill: guitar
Nick Nolan: guitar
Ian Mayo: bass
Tim Pedersen: drums

Recorded at the M.I. studio by T.J. Helmerich. Mixed by Dennis Beck with the help of the R.I.T. class of November 1996.

Danny thanks:
Wendy B. for always going way above and beyond the call of duty, and Mori Domae for always doing his homework.

Nick thanks:
My wife Hiko (for everything), and Rob and Mick at Hoshino (for the great Talman).

Danny and Nick searching for that elusive lick.

GUITAR NOTATION LEGEND

Guitar Music can be notated three different ways: on a *musical staff*, in *tablature*, and in *rhythm slashes*.

RHYTHM SLASHES are written above the staff. Strum chords in the rhythm indicated. Use the chord diagrams found at the top of the first page of the transcription for the appropriate chord voicings. Round noteheads indicate single notes.

THE MUSICAL STAFF shows pitches and rhythms and is divided by bar lines into measures. Pitches are named after the first seven letters of the alphabet.

TABLATURE graphically represents the guitar fingerboard. Each horizontal line represents a string, and each number represents a fret.

Notes:

Strings:

4th string, 2nd fret   1st & 2nd strings open, played together   open D chord

HALF-STEP BEND: Strike the note and bend up 1/2 step.

WHOLE-STEP BEND: Strike the note and bend up one step.

GRACE NOTE BEND: Strike the note and bend up as indicated. The first note does not take up any time.

SLIGHT (MICROTONE) BEND: Strike the note and bend up 1/4 step.

BEND AND RELEASE: Strike the note and bend up as indicated, then release back to the original note. Only the first note is struck.

PRE-BEND: Bend the note as indicated, then strike it.

VIBRATO: The string is vibrated by rapidly bending and releasing the note with the fretting hand.

WIDE VIBRATO: The pitch is varied to a greater degree by vibrating with the fretting hand.

HAMMER-ON: Strike the first (lower) note with one finger, then sound the higher note (on the same string) with another finger by fretting it without picking.

PULL-OFF: Place both fingers on the notes to be sounded. Strike the first note and without picking, pull the finger off to sound the second (lower) note.

LEGATO SLIDE: Strike the first note and then slide the same fret-hand finger up or down to the second note. The second note is not struck.

SHIFT SLIDE: Same as legato slide, except the second note is struck.

TRILL: Very rapidly alternate between the notes indicated by continuously hammering on and pulling off.

TAPPING: Hammer ("tap") the fret indicated with the pick-hand index or middle finger and pull off to the note fretted by the fret hand.

NATURAL HARMONIC: Strike the note while the fret-hand lightly touches the string directly over the fret indicated.

PINCH HARMONIC: The note is fretted normally and a harmonic is produced by adding the edge of the thumb or the tip of the index finger of the pick hand to the normal pick attack.

PICK SCRAPE: The edge of the pick is rubbed down (or up) the string, producing a scratchy sound.

MUFFLED STRINGS: A percussive sound is produced by laying the fret hand across the string(s) without depressing, and striking them with the pick hand.

PALM MUTING: The note is partially muted by the pick hand lightly touching the string(s) just before the bridge.

RAKE: Drag the pick across the strings indicated with a single motion.

TREMOLO PICKING: The note is picked as rapidly and continuously as possible.

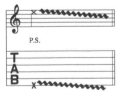

VIBRATO BAR DIVE AND RETURN: The pitch of the note or chord is dropped a specified number of steps (in rhythm) then returned to the original pitch.

VIBRATO BAR SCOOP: Depress the bar just before striking the note, then quickly release the bar.

VIBRATO BAR DIP: Strike the note and then immediately drop a specified number of steps, then release back to the original pitch.

MUSICIANS INSTITUTE PRESS is the official series of Southern California's renowned music school, Musicians Institute. MI instructors, some of the finest musicians in the world, share their vast knowledge and experience with you – no matter what your current level. For guitar, bass, drums, vocals, and keyboards, MI Press offers the finest music curriculum for higher learning through a variety of series:

ESSENTIAL CONCEPTS
Designed from MI core curriculum programs.

MASTER CLASS
Designed from MI elective courses.

PRIVATE LESSONS
Tackle a variety of topics "one-on one" with MI faculty instructors.

GUITAR

Acoustic Artistry
by Evan Hirschelman • Private Lessons
00695922 Book/Online Audio $19.99

Advanced Scale Concepts & Licks for Guitar
by Jean Marc Belkadi • Private Lessons
00695298 Book/CD Pack $19.99

All-in-One Guitar Soloing Course
by Daniel Gilbert & Beth Marlis
00217709 Book/Online Media $29.99

Blues/Rock Soloing for Guitar
by Robert Calva • Private Lessons
00695680 Book/CD Pack $19.99

Blues Guitar Soloing
by Keith Wyatt • Master Class
00695132 Book/Online Audio $29.99

Blues Rhythm Guitar
by Keith Wyatt • Master Class
00695131 Book/Online Audio $19.99

Dean Brown
00696002 DVD $29.95

Chord Progressions for Guitar
by Tom Kolb • Private Lessons
00695664 Book/Online Audio $19.99

Chord Tone Soloing
by Barrett Tagliarino • Private Lessons
00695855 Book/Online Audio $24.99

Chord-Melody Guitar
by Bruce Buckingham • Private Lessons
00695646 Book/Online Audio $19.99

Classical & Fingerstyle Guitar Techniques
by David Oakes • Master Class
00695171 Book/Online Audio $19.99

Classical Themes for Electric Guitar
by Jean Marc Belkadi • Private Lessons
00695806 Book/CD Pack $15.99

Country Guitar
by Al Bonhomme • Master Class
00695661 Book/Online Audio $19.99

Diminished Scale for Guitar
by Jean Marc Belkadi • Private Lessons
00695227 Book/CD Pack $14.99

Essential Rhythm Guitar
by Steve Trovato • Private Lessons
00695181 Book/CD Pack $16.99

Exotic Scales & Licks for Electric Guitar
by Jean Marc Belkadi • Private Lessons
00695860 Book/CD Pack $16.95

Funk Guitar
by Ross Bolton • Private Lessons
00695419 Book/CD Pack $15.99

Guitar Basics
by Bruce Buckingham • Private Lessons
00695134 Book/Online Audio $17.99

Guitar Fretboard Workbook
by Barrett Tagliarino • Essential Concepts
00695712 . . . . $19.99

Guitar Hanon
by Peter Deneff • Private Lessons
00695321 . . . . $14.99

Guitar Lick•tionary
by Dave Hill • Private Lessons
00695482 Book/CD Pack $21.99

Guitar Soloing
by Dan Gilbert & Beth Marlis • Essential Concepts
00695190 Book/CD Pack $22.99

Harmonics
by Jamie Findlay • Private Lessons
00695169 Book/CD Pack $13.99

Harmony & Theory
by Keith Wyatt & Carl Schroeder • Essential Concepts
00695169 . . . . $22.99

Introduction to Jazz Guitar Soloing
by Joe Elliott • Master Class
00695161 Book/Online Audio $19.95

Jazz Guitar Chord System
by Scott Henderson • Private Lessons
00695291 . . . . $12.99

Jazz Guitar Improvisation
by Sid Jacobs • Master Class
00217711 Book/Online Media $19.99

Jazz, Rock & Funk Guitar
by Dean Brown • Private Lessons
00217690 Book/Online Media $19.99

Jazz-Rock Triad Improvising
by Jean Marc Belkadi • Private Lessons
00695361 Book/CD Pack $15.99

Latin Guitar
by Bruce Buckingham • Master Class
00695379 Book/Online Audio $17.99

Lead Sheet Bible
by Robin Randall & Janice Peterson • Private Lessons
00695130 Book/CD Pack $22.99

Liquid Legato
by Allen Hinds • Private Lessons
00696656 Book/Online Audio $16.99

Modern Jazz Concepts for Guitar
by Sid Jacobs • Master Class
00695711 Book/CD Pack $16.95

Modern Rock Rhythm Guitar
by Danny Gill • Private Lessons
00695682 Book/Online Audio $19.99

Modes for Guitar
by Tom Kolb • Private Lessons
00695555 Book/Online Audio $18.99

Music Reading for Guitar
by David Oakes • Essential Concepts
00695192 . . . . $19.99

The Musician's Guide to Recording Acoustic Guitar
by Dallan Beck • Master Class
00695505 Book/CD Pack $13.99

Outside Guitar Licks
by Jean Marc Belkadi • Private Lessons
00695697 Book/CD Pack $16.99

Power Plucking
by Dale Turner • Private Lesson
00695962 Book/CD Pack $19.95

Progressive Tapping Licks
by Jean Marc Belkadi • Private Lessons
00695748 Book/CD Pack $17.99

Rhythm Guitar
by Bruce Buckingham & Eric Paschal • Essential Concepts
00695188 Book $19.99
00114559 Book/Online Audio $24.99
00695909 DVD $19.95

Rhythmic Lead Guitar
by Barrett Tagliarino • Private Lessons
00110263 Book/Online Audio $19.99

Rock Lead Basics
by Nick Nolan & Danny Gill • Master Class
00695144 Book/Online Audio $18.99
00695910 DVD $19.95

Rock Lead Performance
by Nick Nolan & Danny Gill • Master Class
00695278 Book/Online Audio $17.99

Rock Lead Techniques
by Nick Nolan & Danny Gill • Master Class
00695146 Book/Online Audio $16.99

Shred Guitar
by Greg Harrison • Master Class
00695977 Book/CD Pack $19.99

Slap & Pop Technique for Guitar
by Jean Marc Bekaldi • Private Lessons
00695645 Book/CD Pack $17.99

Solo Slap Guitar
by Jude Gold • Master Class
00139556 Book/Online Video $19.99

Technique Exercises for Guitar
by Jean Marc Belkadi • Private Lessons
00695913 Book/CD Pack $15.99

Texas Blues Guitar
by Robert Calva • Private Lessons
00695340 Book/Online Audio $17.99

Ultimate Guitar Technique
by Bill LaFleur • Private Lessons
00695863 Book/Online Audio $22.99

Prices, contents, and availability subject to change without notice.

HAL•LEONARD®
7777 W. BLUEMOUND RD. P.O. BOX 13819 MILWAUKEE, WI 53213
www.halleonard.com